Jerusalem, beloved

Jerusalem, beloved

To Beth
so lovely to be
in Goshen,
thank for the
warm Mennonite
hospitality!
Di Brandt

Goshen
Jan '03

Di Brandt

TURNSTONE PRESS

Turnstone Press
607-100 Arthur Street
Winnipeg, Manitoba
Canada   R3B 1H3

Turnstone Press gratefully acknowledges the assistance of
the Canada Council and the Manitoba Arts Council.

Some of these poems have appeared previously in *Arc,*
Canadian Forum, Contemporary Verse 2, Drop Out (Rhinocerotic
Press 1993), *Moosehead Anthology, Prairire Fire, Prairie Schooner,*
Quarry Magazine, Signs of the Times (Christian Peacemaker Team
Newsletter), *The New Quarterly,* and *Women and Violence*
(League of Canadian Poets Feminist Caucus Living Archives
1992, ed. Sarah Klassen). The Jerusalem poems were featured
on *Speaking Volumes, Arts Encounters and Aircraft* (CBC Radio),
and *The Jewish Connection* (Videon TV).

Cover image: "Jerusalem Heritage," by Taysir Sharaf

Design: Manuela Dias

This book was printed and bound in Canada by
Kromar Printing for Turnstone Press

Second printing: February 1996

Canadian Cataloguing in Publication Data

Brandt, Di

Jerusalem, beloved

Poems.
ISBN 0-88801-196-2

I. Title

PS8553.R2953J4 1995   C811'.54   C95-920114-9
PR9199.3.B7295J4 1995

for Kathy

table of contents

Jerusalem, beloved

blue light, falling around us

those of us who have daughters

acknowledgments

with thanks to Kathy Bergen for the incredible tour of occupied Palestine, shortly after the Persian Gulf War in 1991. thanks to Lisa & Ali for coming along & sharing laughter & keen insights. Gene Stoltzfus generously invited me to join his energetic Christian Peacemaker Team study group in Bethlehem & Gaza. thank you for the wonderful hospitality from many people in Palestine and Israel, including Father Elias Chacour in Ibillin, Mustafa al-Kurd & Helga Baumgarten, Jan & Samir Abu Shakrah, & Suha Hindiye & Maged Mani in Jerusalem, Jocelyne Talbot of O.C.S.D. (Organization de Canadien Solidarite et Developement in Palestine), Muhana Arab near Bethlehem, Gidon Spiro of Yesh Guvul (organization of Israeli soldiers resisting serving in the Occupied Territories), The Women in Black of Jerusalem, Amos Gvritz of Kibbutz Shefayim, Dr. Haider Abdul Shafi in Gaza, Sahar Khalifeh & the women at the Women's Center in Nablus, Mark Taylor in Ramallah, Jamel Salkud, Izzat Ahazzawi, & Almutawakel Taha of the Palestinian Writers' Union in Jerusalem, members of the Rapprochement Center in Bethlehem, Georges Rioux & Michel de Saliberry of the Canadian Embassy in Tel Aviv, & the Saadeh family at the Jerusalem Hotel. thanks to all of you for sharing your vision of Jerusalem & the surrounding countryside with me.

thanks also to Jamie Hutchison, Christine Dulat, & Manuela Dias of Turnstone Press for creating a beautiful book, Taysir Sharaf for lending me his painting "Jerusalem Heritage" for the cover, & David Arnason for editing

this book was made possible through the generous support of the Canada Council, the Manitoba Arts Council, & Arts Encounters (CBC Radio)

And the stones of the poor of Jerusalem
Guard the roses
—Mustafa al-Kurd

When I am dead, even then,
I will still love you, I will wait in these poems,
When I am dead, even then
I am still listening to you.
—Muriel Rukeyser

Jerusalem, beloved

Jerusalem, the golden, city of my dreams,
dreaming, how i waited all my life for you,
to find you, resplendent, in the sun, your
white stones crying, with joy, Jerusalem,
beloved, lying in the Mediterranean sun,
filled with love, delirious with love, *lift up
your heart & sing*, my heart dancing, how i
longed for you, all my life, your streets
paved with gold, & children playing, your
diamond studded gates, your rooftops filled
with women, dancing, & flowers in their
hair, the tables laden, heavy, the air filled
with music, & feasting, my love, how i
longed for you, dreaming, my arms aching,
from the day of my birth, my birthgiving,
filled with pangs of hunger & remembering,
how i longed for you, my love, how long,
oh how long i waited for you

nothing's like that, like the dream. there are
soldiers with guns at the airport in Frankfurt,
we're being searched, our bags, our underwear,
towels, teddy bears, nothing's safe, not even
the children's things, everything is dangerous,
cameras hide weapons, bottled water's poison,
the soldiers in uniform looking just like Nazis,
here we are, in the war zone, suddenly,
everything familiar, dangerous, the light on
the wall too bright, & distant, the room
suddenly big, dangerous, faces swimming,
why are you going to Jerusalem, she asks,
disinterested, distant, scrutinizing, *why
are you here?*

i wanted the road to Jerusalem strewn with palm
branches, i wanted the sun slanting its rays
over the horizon to touch everything red gold,
i wanted to hear angels singing.

Kathy is two hours late, sweaty, embarrassed,
fuming: the taxi-driver was stopped at the gate,
his third time today, for questioning, the
car searched, in detail, again, everything dismantled,
even the seats, it's hard to earn a living like this,
every day, eighteen-year-old boys with
submachine guns, pointing, shouting, prodding
at you, full of contempt, three hours wasted
this afternoon, just a formality, state security, every
Palestinian a potential terrorist, in their eyes, i'm
weary of this life, i just want to earn a living, go
home to my family, eat, sleep, *iwa*, it's crazy
here, i'm weary of this life.

i didn't want it to be like this, a nightmare in living
colour, all around us, violence built over this
beautiful, familiar landscape, like a temple, like
a church, soldiers on every corner, & i implicated
in it, a Canadian, North American, tourist, rich
enough to buy a plane ticket over the Atlantic,
innocent bystander, onlooker, nothing is innocent,
here, where even the stones are crying, look, look,
what is happening here. i didn't want it to be like
this.

where did they go, when the machines came to tear
down their houses, uproot the olive trees, so
carefully tended, for hundreds of years, where did
they go, the people of this village, that has no name
now, wringing their hands, wailing, holding their
children, tight, sobbing, this is how we build parks,
in Israel, how we build them in Canada, too, it's how
we build them in Canada, too.

this is what i want to remember, the mauve evening
light around us as we sat & smoked, the Arabic
coffee brought to us *gratis* by the Palestinian waiter,
the hills across the sea of Galilee, iridescent,
shimmering in the evening sun, the sound of the
waves as we caught up with each others' lives, so
many years flowing away between us & yet, each
time we see each other across these continents, the
same feeling of warmth, connection, you're my
best, oldest friend, she says, reaching her hand across
the table, this is what i want to remember, this
perfect suspended moment, the candles flickering
against the darkening sea, the hills blue black across
the sea of Galilee

well dressed, fashionable tourists sauntering by,
guns slung over their shoulders, casually, settlers
with German & American accents, armed with their
own suffering, immune, & one young man or
another, crazed with grief over the lost villages of
his ancestors, his father, stripped of house & home,
the olive grove he played in as a child cut down, the
old man wandering about the countryside, dazed,
one young man throwing stones, tomorrow he will
be dead, i do not want to know the politics of
recolonizing this beautiful, shocking country, the
brutal, fisted truth of these buildings, these stones,
how they cry out to us as we pass by, the barbaric
reality of real estate, here by the sea, where Jesus
might have walked, sandal footed, in Tiberius,
the accumulated violence of centuries, blossoming,
incandescent, in the streets, here, by this radiant sea,
the same old stupid history, as usual, being made.

i have seen everything before, the street sloping
down to the old city, the women sitting cross legged
with their figs, & grape leaves, & red peppers, young
men calling out their wares, bracelets, sandals, bread,
satte, hey, lady, one minute, i show you, the best
sandals in Jerusalem, the best price, the old women
passing by, their heads covered in black, white, their
long embroidered dresses, jewelry, the market,
bustling in the sun, everyone shouting, one more sale
before noon, everyone closing for the strike, no
shopping in the afternoons in the old city, since the
Intifada, sorry, ma'am, everything's closed.

my old fear grabbing me here, in the market, swiftly,
unable to think, *danger,* everything's too loud, what's
happening, where am i, my children, can't think,
can't breathe, where are they, where am i, how did i
get here?

there are no words in me for Gaza, for what i saw
in Gaza, the eyes of the women lining up at the
hospital for milk, with their babies & small
children, their eyes looking at me, another North
American tourist with nothing to offer, except
terrible pity, & shame, shame at my innocence,
my stupid privilege, i never imagined such a place,
i could have been born here, & thought this is what
the world is like, these narrow streets filled with
flies & cowdung, shacks made of sheet metal &
bare wooden boards, the path to the beach littered
with barbed wire & abandoned jeeps, & grey sand,
how long does it take to forget, the soldiers at the
door, the women screaming, the broken china,
embroidered tablecloths flapping in the wind,
blood running from the father's mouth, how long
does it take to forget, the darkness in this woman's
eyes, the children hiding rocks in their hands on
the way to school, these two will not come home
tonight, their shins broken by soldiers in the street,
these eyes, the long long sorrow in them, these
women's eyes, looking at me

(the children on Main Street in Winnipeg who will be
missing tonight, Colin, eating white glue by the
bowlful at Dufferin School, in kindergarten, what's
the point of sticking bits of wood together when your
stomach is howling, his dark eyes & fine skin, Carla
& James, stabbed in their beds with a kitchen knife
by their father, putting them out of their misery, the
children tell each other in the schoolyard, blond hair
matted across the sheets, the thirteen-year-old girl
behind the Concert Hall, shivering in her thin jacket
& blue jeans, waiting for a five dollar trick in thirty
below weather, who's responsible for this, who made
the rules in this city, that i love, the streets lined with
trees, the cry at the heart of it, a woman camped in
her teepee at the Legislative Grounds, through the
summer, pleading for protection for her children,
who's responsible for this?

when you told me about the Wall, where the women
go to pray at dawn, sighing for God, lips kissing
stone, you didn't tell me how small it was, dwarfed
by new buildings, & the courtyard, & bearded men,
& soldiers surrounding it, pointing guns at the sky,
at passersby, requiring permits of every Palestinian
who wants to visit the mosque, just around the corner,
to pray, you didn't tell me about the shooting in
October at the mosque, the sun flashing against its
golden dome, women & children scattering in the
square, Auni's thirteen-year-old sister hit in the
shoulder, blood everywhere, the soldiers firing berserk
into the crowd, panic, you didn't tell me how fragile,
how tenuous this place of praying is, this broken piece
of promised land, how unholy the ceremonies
surrounding this ravaged bride, this place of
mourning, the women praying here at dawn & Auni,
shivering, crying in the street, *they won't be happy
until they've taken everything, they would like us, all
dead*

a busload of silly Christians, with silly hats, touring
the Holy Land with Bibles & cameras, trying to match
the names in the Book with actual places, seeing only
what the tour guide tells them to see, what kind of
pilgrimage is that? how Jesus would have wept to
see them, how they walk blindly through the streets,
like stupid people, seeing, hearing nothing, *listen,*
i want to shout at them, this is a place of revolution,
where the old crashes against the new, this is a place
where hope dies & is reborn, where the rough
beast slouching toward Bethlehem is transformed,
overnight, into something miraculous, a fantastic
creature, with wings. but that isn't what you want,
is it, it's the same stories, repeated over & over, the
slaying of the Midianites, the crucifixion, high priests
chanting, the litanies of the dead, look around you,
look around you, see the women crying in the streets,
for their dead sons, shot by Israeli/American soldiers,
it's what you want, isn't it, Armageddon, for your
bloodthirsty Old Testament God, your fisted, armoured
hearts, self hatred, your old accumulated baby rage

how long does it take to forget a murder in your
house, behind a closed door, without a sound, no
words said, the hanging in a field your great
grandmother watched as a little girl, her face pushed
against her father's sleeve, a heretic slow burning at
the end of August in the town square? how long
does the body remember the bullet, where it graced
the flesh, the cells burned, blue black, where it
entered skin, nerve endings charred, trembling?
how long does it take to forget a gas chamber filled
with naked, terrified, bearded men, the roomful
of women, the accused, sentenced to burning, a
soldier's rifle under the chin, cocked, the soldier's
hand, shaking, full of hatred, shame, rage?

this black ball we carry around inside us, this
darkness, this red flaming sea, how it comes back
to us, this violence, to haunt us, a ghost, the devil, the
enemy, how it yearns, like tree roots, to take hold, to
flower in us, like branches & leaves:

the body's humiliation, trembling, how it stays in
the air, long after the body is gone, dismembered, the
spirit seeking revenge—or is it comforting it wants,
remembering, shaking, grieving, so we will not do it
again, to someone else, the way it was done to us, so
that the flowering can be trembling, beautiful, wise,
as newborn children are, instead of wrath?

you can see it in the eyes of the waitresses, shop
keepers, tourists sauntering by. the dark place
behind the eyes where the lie is held, knowledge
twisted into forgetting, truth knotted up, inscrutable,
closed like a fist, ghosts leaping out at us, at every
corner, between these neatly renovated cobbled
streets, so many centuries of gathered hurt—

the pretence of sanctuary behind guns, & machines,
the romance of white American military might.
Goliath. Rambo. Saddam Hussein. George Bush.

the old fear crying out.

thirty people shot in the head & chest, in Nablus,
the streets emptied by soldiers, a fifteen-year-old
girl with two children & another on the way, a girl
bride, with wide brown eyes, startled, stumbling
across the street, bartered, in the name of Allah,
against all this suffering, to a thirty-five-year-old
merchant, she will die of old age at forty, & grief,
stumbling across the street, through tear gas &
gunsmoke, her boys in wheelchairs, her daughters
crazy with grief, no, no, this isn't happening, this
isn't my life, no.

Bassam's dark eyes follow me through the courtyard,
from the kitchen to the hotel gate & back again, his
dark eyes filled with sadness, hunger, love. yesterday
when he handed me the key, his fingers made a little
circle in my left palm, grazing the skin there. my hand
remembered his touch all day. this morning, he brings
me hot tea with mint leaves, & pita cut in pieces. later,
when i return, he will be sitting here, under the vine
leaves, next to the fountain, in the dark. he will bring
me wine, or beer, whatever i ask.

the romance of otherness, his dark hair & skin, his
sadness, his foreign smile. this beautiful old hotel.
whatever i ask. does he flirt like this with all the
guests, in front of his brother & cousins? does he
dream of finding a wife, of falling in love? does he
lust after a stranger's skin, for a night, secretly (as i
do), no strings attached, just lips, hands, mouth, thighs,
not caring about afterwards, what people might say?
does he wish to create scandal, leave this country with
its strict old fashioned rules, this besieged, terrified
city? does he dream of Canada, as i once dreamed of
here?

Bassam, Bassam, this poem is for you, your impossible
love, your eyes, that followed me around wherever
i went, in Jerusalem, your sadness, your dark eyes.
this poem is for you.

we're drinking wine on the terrace of Aladin
Restaurant in Jaffa, built on a rock overlooking the
sea, where thieves were drawn & quartered once, &
hung in caves, & a reluctant prophet was spit out,
beached by a whale. a magic lamp.

this was the house of a well-to-do Palestinian
merchant not long ago, you can still see bits of Arabic
motifs, arabesques & scrolls, painted on the walls,
rich carpets hung between arched doorways, Israeli
"artifacts."

the menu is in English, the prices high, inflated for
tourists. across the street a mosque, newly converted
into a Western style discotheque, blares canned rock
music at passersby.

a sign at the waterfront reads:

The Old Jaffa Development Corporation
Located here at the structural remains of
the Jewish house known as "Dar el-Yahud";
acquired in 390 C.E. by Isaiah Ajimen, a Jew from
Constantinople and converted into a
Hostel Ikhani for Jewish pilgrims who
disembarked at Jaffa. A part of the
building also served as a synagogue. Thus
Jewish settlement in Jaffa was renewed.

acquired, converted, occupied, settled, stolen,
appropriated, translated, destroyed, developed.
renewed.

here, in the desert, where everything comes together,
& history is undone, time rolls up into old scrolls,
bits of parchment, brittle, scattering in wind, stories
crumble like walls into sand, silence, old stones, bits
of bones, gritty against your feet, here where
temptation is everything, because the Word means
nothing, is emptied out, the heart listens to itself,
crying, the foxes in the desert have holes, the birds
in the air have nests.

Kathy says, don't let the children out of sight, there
have been kidnappings, settlers on the West Bank,
my stomach screaming briefly its old scream, &,
here they are, blond & brown hair gleaming, in the
sun, with their cameras & sandals, laughing, teasing,
my daughters, they've found a cave with two arched
doorways, black, just big enough to sit in, take a
picture of us, mom, see, they say, laughing, these are
our houses, *smile.*

let me tell you about Muhana, son of Salmon, who
lives in a bus, on the edge of his family's estate,
which housed a mansion once, & a thousand olive
trees, on a hillside overlooking Bethlehem. let me
tell you about this proud & stubborn man, how he
served us stuffed zucchini & lemonade, graciously,
smiling, as we sat on old couches, under a fig tree,
now his living room. his 46 dunams of land, prime
property, sloping down toward West Jerusalem,
worth half a million US, the title transferred illegally
to an Israeli/American businessman in California.

his left shoulder, his left thigh, where electric wires
burned through the flesh, in prison, killing the nerves.

his sister, who went crazy & jumped to her death
from a tree. his old father, who died of cold, & a
broken heart.

the mother, tortured in prison, her eyes gouged out
by prison guards.

his 46 dunams of land, the heartbreak of it, every
olive tree cut down, the rich topsoil scooped up at
night & carried away in trucks, his father's house,
the family mansion, centuries old, razed to a heap
of rubble in an hour. a twelve-year-old boy seated
on a bulldozer, unaccountable.

the mother, tortured in prison, her eyes gouged out
by prison guards.

how he lies awake at night, waiting for soldiers.
how he dreams of heaven.

Muhana, with his smile & his proud, stubborn
spirit, sewing clothes for people in his battered old
bus, for a handful of shekels. Muhana, the
gracious, the steadfast, the loyal son, proudly
displaying his sign to visitors:

We Love Kathy, And We Love Our Land.

descending into the valley of the Dead Sea the sun is
hot, hot, the air is heavy, the sand around us faceless,
voiceless, there is no life here, only a narrow paved
road, with no cars, & red rock, towering, brown
goats rambling in its crevices, centuries of silence
breaking, echoing around us, our necks & foreheads
drenched in sweat (come in under the shadow of this
red rock), down, down under the shadow, into the
valley of the dead sea

sparkling in the sun with the light of a million
diamonds, blue, turquoise, silver, children playing in
the water, & it's true, you can float! you could read a
book sitting here, feet pointing to shore, bobbing up
& down, the taste of salt on our lips, stinging our
eyes, the sand black & gritty against our feet, legs,
the children arranging themselves like Hollywood
starlets on their towels, it only lasts a moment, sun's
much too hot (looking into the heart of light)

a swimmer walks by, & offers us a ball of mud,
black, cool, soothing on the skin, people come here
from all over the world to bathe in the healing waters
of this beautiful blue sea, this salt sea, this sea
of love with its black shore, *ahava*

so hard to uproot the prickly pear, it just keeps
growing, pushing its roots into dry ground, needles
bristling, against outsiders, marauders, thieves, a
good hedge against strangers, permanent protection,
you might say, long after the houses have been
looted, trashed, bulldozed to rubble, a heap of stones
on a bare hillside, witness the prickly pear! guarding
the place of its master, calling out to passersby, the
precise memory of sobbing, clinging, hand wringing
not long ago, here, on this empty slope, beside a
freeway, this innocent looking spot, these sudden
splashes of green, impossible to uproot or poison,
these giant bulbs sprouting tiny desert swords,
poised to stab

this is a country of soldiers, he says, & boys & old
men, locked in combat, running through the streets,
shooting bullets, throwing stones, tossing dice into
the air, exchanging words, exclaiming, each against
the hostile universe, their claim, this is the way it is,
he says, almost shrugging, in a world traversed by
deadly currents, passion running through men's veins,
spilling onto streets, ricocheting against the walls of
houses, echoing & echoing

every Friday the women gather in Jerusalem,
wearing black, holding roses instead of guns, to
protest their sons & brothers becoming killers, their
husbands coming home at night, tight lipped, tossing
in bed, feverish, moaning, their aging fathers mean
& hard with anger, shouting, arguing with everyone,
with God, the women silent against them, wearing
black, holding roses, heartsick, against the tide of
blood flowing through Israel, is this the kind of
homeland we wanted, is this the kind of sons &
daughters we wanted, hard, embittered, scarred?

& in Nablus, the women gather in houses to teach
each other to write, & think, & speak, & cook, &
sew, to bandage up the legs & arms & eyes of their
wounded young, thinking, when will this end, this
stupid, crazy occupation, when will it end?

(after Semcha Jakobovici's film, *Deadly Currents*)

the trees of Jerusalem, so much sadder than
Winnipeg trees, quieter, lodged between stone
walls, overlooking the noises of the street, so
much older, darker green, drawn into themselves,
no longer listening for gunshots, screams, a body
being dragged over stones, they have heard this
all before, so many times, dreaming of orchards,
birds, music, listen, the *ud* playing, plaintively,
in the distance, women dancing, ever so softly,
on rooftops, remembering, the promises of their
mothers, their first lovers, reconstructing, lightly,
the fantasy of heaven

crossing the river Jordan in a silver Palestinian
rent-a-car, insured against stone throwing on the
West Bank, the manager assured us, though not
against army tanks, the bridge is made of old logs
which rattle as we bump across, &, *is this it?* is
this all it was? the mythological river, filled with
saints *going through to the other side*, the eternal
river sung into our blood, this dark narrow ditch
overhung with trees, & reeds, this ordinary river,
less interesting than the Assiniboine in Winnipeg,
& me having to pee, & is this what heaven is?
such an ordinary crossing in broad daylight, to a
landscape much like the one you left, your dreams
the only happiness, what you brought with you,
the ache in your belly, your feet, throat, a lifetime
of thirst, how to drink, make the dream happen,
without violence, such a strange birthing, this
crossing over, imagining into promised land?

❦

waking up in Jerusalem, the voice on the minaret,
the call to prayers, the cat on the police station roof,
yowling, do they torture cats here, too, the street below
our window, bustling since dawn, women carrying
baskets, boys with carts, the donkey at the corner,
nodding, half asleep, its tail flicking at flies, the sun
already high, heat rising from the street like steam,
the men next door shouting at each other, the cement
wall they're building another two feet higher, the
rooftops white, gleaming, the smell of coffee
downstairs, dishes clattering, &, *i can't take this*,
i can't really be here, in this magical city, this isn't
really a place, i want to go home, escape back into
language, the dream, where i came from, i don't
want to be here, among all these stones, centuries
crashing around me, i want to go back to the prairies,
to emptiness, words circling around absence, the
straight horizon, home

blue light, falling around us

three women are sitting at a table in a cottage by the
sea, eating stewed mussels, noisily, slurping the soft meat
from its shell. the moon's risen over the dark water,
dotting the waves with flecks of light. the grass outside
the cottage is singing, alive with crickets & frogs. all
around the room are small clay figurines, handmade
goddesses with full breasts, bellies, vulvas, squatting on
the ground in positions of ecstasy. the women push
back their chairs, they know exactly what it has
cost each of them to remember, stay alive, speak to each
other, as women. they lift cups of wine & tea & toast
one another. they understand how radically they are
challenging, changing, remaking history. they are awed
by this thought, but not overwhelmed. across the bay
the munitions factory spews smoke into the air. they
decide to go for a swim.

why you keep on doing it, getting up in the morning,
feeling the pain in your side, the night taste in your
mouth, walking to the door in your bare feet to let
out the dog, wake the children, move into the day's
routine. because the trees outside your window are
splendid, the wind in the branches waves the sky
along, grandly. because the earth under your feet is
there, every morning, solid, profound, hanging in
air, filled with gravity & lightness, keeping you there,
attached, safe, able to walk & dream about blue,
through these troubled times, without flying off into
space, this earth is my home, my body, my mother,
unafraid & so, unutterably, beautiful.

(not wanting to leave Winnipeg in May, the incredible
green, the great lush burst of it, it hurts your eyes, so
many summers sliding into grey, & this time, tuned
precisely to the pulse of spring, its explosion in air,
more beautiful than a million stars, it hurts your
heart, this fragility, the power in it, each blossom
more knowledgeable than any killer, what to do with
it, what to do

today i'm crying for the women of Iraq,
for the weeping, overburdened earth. i'm
crying for our children who are growing
up at river's edge, talking like this:

you should be glad i haven't killed myself or turned
psycho crazy, you should be glad i haven't made the
choices my friends have made, who are stoned all day
long, you should be glad i'm even here, i'm still alive,
i haven't flipped out on the crazy world, full of people
who go around shooting each other, killing off all the
animals, you should be glad i'm here, i'm still alive.

&, i *am* glad they're still here, alive, these beautiful
angry children, wanting so much to grow up but not
into adults & who can blame them. aren't you?

this time i catch myself, falling, through
air, like a star, i am floating, above clouds,
lightly, feathered, against crashing, the old
cry in me a faint echo, distant, receding,
i'm falling, through air, the sun through the
clouds breaking, pink, purple, golden
against the horizon, the sun flecked leaves
trembling, the night air whispering up
from the dark earth, remembering dark,
hush, this time, falling softly, into

the sky, in the forest, that day, all around us,
blue light, falling, on snow, slush, the bare
trees, last year's grass flattened under ice, the
smell of horse turds, melting, buds beginning
to burst, silence, blue light, falling around
us, your face, your eyes, filled with sky, your
hair, flame coloured, apricot, saffron, gold
against the light, sky blue, baby blue, robin's
egg blue, aquamarine, sapphire

if i said it was spectacular, our falling, in April,
through sky, through blue air, into spring, into love,
like meteors, trailing fire & gold dust, if i said it was
quiet, like deer nesting, among trees, nudging each
other with wet noses, their breath making invisible
clouds of warmth against the last snow, if i said i
shook, when you held me, not for ghosts, old
demons, old farts, but for you, for the fresh smart
sting of the real, the liquid spirit of you & me,
golden lava flowing between us, remembering that
first moment, pure energy bursting into blossom,
flame, the world starting over, again, in the
beginning, before words, cells trembling, the first
language, the pull of earth, body, calling out,
touching, breath kicking in

◆

because the windows were falling, & the children
angry, shouting, at the absence of their mother, there,
that minute, on the back steps, to catch them, after
the winter, with impossibly long arms, outstretched,
& she wasn't there—

she *was* there, in the front, on the verandah, thinking
about them, how tall & beautiful they were, almost
women, she was talking about them to her lover,
wanting to make a gift of their anger, the old hurt in
them leaking out, into almost love, it was what she
had to offer, that day, to them, to her, all the old
walls crumbling, beginning to fall down, the way the
light caught on her hand, against purple, amethyst,
too beautiful for words, her heart gasping, scared,
not scared, not scared, knowing love, that way, for
the first time, between women, *mother love*, feet
touching ground, not floating away, not falling, into
black space, unprotected, shelterless—

the house standing solid, the children opening
windows to summer air, sunlight glinting against
amethyst, hands, touching, home

with you all the old wounds, scars in my flesh,
are coming undone, & old grief pouring out, is it
okay with you, lover, this opening, this wild
travel in space, each time we kiss, this hurtling
through black, emptiness, swirling galaxies, to
your warmth, your arms, your mouth, your
singing bones, full of light, here in this bed, this
room, where everything in me is being reborn,
baptized, burnished, golden

& then you were gone, on your bike, & i missed
you, foolishly, like a child, sitting on my verandah,
listening to the trees, the wind ruffling their
branches, tossing them, like hair, wildly, all over
the sky, & i was listening to them in the dark,
rustling, thinking about you, how you were gone,
suddenly, on your bike, in the night, & how i wanted
you, more than anything, just then, next to me, in
my arms, our skin touching, our breath meeting, *oh,*
i wanted you more than anything

so many things i didn't know before i met you:

the ruddy tailed duck with its light blue beak,
paddling around the marsh like a little boat, tall
green marsh grass, phragmites, every blade marked
with the "teeth of Christ" (how he could have got
here, across the ocean, in time for spring, why he
would have wanted to bite every leaf, running
frantically, from clump to clump, tossing his sandals
aside in the mud, what the ruddy ducks might have
thought), every flaming hair on your head crying
out as it's cut, ouch! ouch! don't hurt me! a million
little corpses on the hairdresser's floor, gleaming,
copper & gold, your bluegreen eyes, the time we
burned a book of matches & couldn't get the candles
lit, the almost romance of the daily, with you, miso
soup, your small hands, your skin, dappled,
beautiful

holding you i let fall the thousand knives poised
at the white, washed ceiling of my heart, down
to the basement of my dark red womb—old
guardians, no longer needed, or useful, here, in
this peace zone, with you—

the dropped weapons clatter on the unswept
floor, flash bronze & silver in the dust, stir up
old scars, cut me open, bleeding, darkly, in July,
with old memories, i do not want to remember,
so much blood, opening myself, to you

the rivers of tears i have cried, an ocean, not
enough salt water to wash out this cave, this
temple, this holy place, where you have come,
visitor, bearing gifts, flowers, incense, precious
stones, where every wall is cracking open, to
sky, & sun, welkomen, to these lovely ruins,
these cut rocks, these ancient sacred standing
stones

lovers, slow dancing in the rain

this is it! i've found it at last! nirvana, the Elysian
fields, heaven.

let me spend the rest of my life here, on the banks
of the Saskatchewan, listening, to grass rustling,
geese trumpeting their young, the smell of clover on
the dry wind, last summer's leaves flaming in the
October sun, the air sharp today, reminding of
winter, only, you are not here—your absence tinges
the blue air with silence, in the midst of all this
singing, i hate it, i hate it, how love makes me cry
out in October, against this glorious bursting, of
matter into fire, your spirit on the wind is not
enough, i want flesh, skin, wet tongue against wet
tongue, belly, all the miles between us rolled up into
here & now, heaven exploding in our honeyed
mouths, the blue Saskatchewan rippling against the
breeze, the trees, slowly, turning

yesterday your absence was a hole inside me, today
it's a stone.

funny how nothing, no one there, can feel so heavy,
a granite boulder, heaving against earth & body,
cutting off air. yesterday, i thought i was floating,
free of gravity, nothing to keep me here. now
everything's bloated, swollen, feet & head made of
clay.

the trees are singing in loud whispers, against the
rain. against the night sky, rumbling with heavy
grey clouds, magnificent. but i can't hear them, can
hear only the rush of my own heart, beating itself
silly in the dark, against your absence, your surely
maybe must be coming back.

a granite boulder cracking open to sunlight, to
thinning summer air. tufts of grass growing in its
folds, uninvited, stubborn, against despair.

translating the language of my foreign belly
      to the face & skin that is you:

reaching across

                the grand canyon

our voices in this space

                        echoing

      pursuing/////   /distancing

hello   can i hear you?

          i hear you?

are you there   you there?

     hide & seek

              (peek)

qeoi icpwic'owrfvmev t reit w0ix snd wkjasz
(qeoi icpwic'o wrfvmev t reit w0ix snd wkjasz)

\&

& suddenly, driving down Grant Avenue in Winnipeg,
i'm in Israel again, green army tanks lumbering by,
young soldiers with gleaming smiles, shaven hair, army
berets, how casual they look, how confident, with their
big green toys, death toys, & why not, isn't that what the
movies tell them, when the guns go off, when the
shooting starts, they'll be heroes, center stage, flags
waving, & women swooning, no one talks about the
children with broken legs, their mouths bleeding in a
cement gutter, the old women behind the village
barricade, boiling coffee, the ghosts of the ancestors
hovering, anxious, over their threatened graves, no one
talks about the dead men lurking in their bones, legs shot
off, fingers missing, peacekeeping, we call it, we with
our cars & refrigerators & VCR's, the mothers crying in
their kitchens, the big white fathers hiding in their
offices, with stiff neckties, & collars & throats which
have forgotten how to laugh, or cry, or feel the
trembling of their sons, at night, across the water, in the
dark, in Cypress, in Sarajevo, the muffled beating of
their own dark hearts

each cell, at 2 a.m., listening to the whisper,
the slight knocking of death at the door, every
nerve, every fiber & tissue, on edge, against
time, rustling, the inevitable opening into
darkness, the white white white light of each
beginning, & end, this is it, the cosmos,
playing its ancient music, slowly, the spheres
rubbing together in their great turning, how it
enters us like a stranger, uninvited, piercing us
with its large darkness, like ice, knocking the
wind out of us, completely, so surprised, not
recognizing the universe, our mother, coming
back for us, reaching out her arms, her hot
woman's love burning through each trembling
cell, calling out to us, her dark liquid lullaby
flowing through us, & up, & up, back to the
stars, mother, queen of heaven, Most Beloved,
home

those of us who have daughters

〽

Earth falling, empty, silent.

(cicadas buzzing in the trees, endless hot summer
afternoons. fireflies, darting through the air like little
meteors, after dark, little airplanes you could catch in
your hands, half a dozen at a time & let go in a spray
of light. frogs, dozens of them, croaking, hopping on
the driveway at dusk, after rain, like little wizened
men. the children leaping among them, delighted.
two dozen kinds of birdsong on every yard, flashes of
red, yellow, blue, all summer long among the
evergreens.)

two loons on the lake, this summer, instead of twenty.
one family of ducks. two fireflies in the forest,
tonight, in all these trees. no moths, snakes, frogs, no
cantankerous beetles. no owls.

the falling, silent.

the poem no one will ever see.

the poem made out of darkness, so dark, it
swallows up the light, the white page, the eye
seeing, the i, seeing. energy turned inside out,
collapsing into itself, a swirling vortex, the black
hole, danger.

i want to be the first astronaut to go into the black
hole, she said. but i wouldn't want you to do that,
i said, if you go into the black hole you can't come
back out. well then, she said, i'm going to be the
first astronaut to go into the black hole & come
back out again. alive.

the black hole, turning, swirling, dangerous, the
poem no one will ever see, breaking, scattering,
leaking onto the page, the i, seeing, time flowing
backwards, the tree's leaves lifting themselves
from the damp grass, onto green stems, sap
running back to the ground, every black branch
pulling itself back into seedlings, young, tender,
the dark turning itself inside out, bowing,
elegantly, toward the light.

—*for Ali*

so, brother, little brother, big brother, made kin
by killing hands, no, not so, by our remembering
them, spinning around the room, through space
& time, to other rooms, & galaxies, blue black
surround, & flash of light around our heads,
glowing, white, against the night, those hands,
pressed down, hard, against our childish throats,
the helpless father rage in them, the bruise
beneath the skin, the scream locked in the cells,
blood hammering through the brain, how long it's
taking, little brother, to remember, to forget, how
many hours, years, spinning, dancing, screaming,
letting go—

& you, where are you this sweet, scented
summer night, & are there blossoms dripping on
your street, & are your hands unclenching still,
the knife in them glinting silver against the light,
the lost parts of our hundred selves shivering
their way back into skin, trailing stardust,
moondust, hot coals, blooming in our blood

—*for Robert Priest*

without skin, we are sitting together in Sarah's
living room, listening to each other's words, &
music, & images in photographs, collages, the
dream in them, the open mouth, screaming, the
dance of light on shells, fish heads, beads, rolling
off the page, onto the floor, our bare feet, the
bones in them gleaming, white, against the brown
rug, shaggy & ruffled like teddy bear fur, hard to
listen to viola, like this, unbuttoned, the sound of
wind translated into notes, not human, black sky
funnelling into light, the wings of the little brown
bird, found dead on the sidewalk, folded over the
little white owl, the sound of our mothers' fears
whispering in the spaces between the notes,
shivering, & we are held like this, human against
the night, bathed in the warmth of our skinless
selves, our smiling bellies, our ungarrisoned
unmuffled beating hearts

—*for Sarah Turner*

letting out the old dangerous words, with you,
tonight, here in this soft winter light, easing into
dark, the snow just as new & white as it was then,
ringed with stars & clear sky, before it all flew
apart, into fists & gunshots, & endless stomach
aches, the years i've waited, darling, for these
wounds to be undone, these old tears to be cried,
& you here with me, *like angels*, singing, imagine,
middle aged women like us, with our softening
bellies, & seasoned thighs, our voices carrying
across the miles, deep, melodic, the years rolling
up between us like Crêpes Suzette, dribbling
orange juice & honey, with a little cognac, down
our chins

—*for Rosie*

so, Marie, i've started hearing them, just like you
said, voices in the landscape, ancestors, yours &
mine, the spirits of our grandmothers, singing,
except, who would want to hear them, their outrage,
& anger, their great bright grief, how they weep &
tear their hair in the wind, tossing against every tree,
it's hard to listen, but i must, now that i've called
them up, out of the night, Sarah, & Eva, & Anna
Maria, & those others, whose names i don't know,
wailing their songs in my ears, but at least they have
voices, at least they can rage, their anger rising like
flames in prairie wind, remembering dust & buffalo
skin & white bones, a creaking old ship bulkily
plowing through ocean waves, the straight horizon,
blue, grey, white, grey, the children hungry, crying,
nausea, morning sickness, fainting, & before that,
before that, before that, remembering, an empty
field, a black cross, a forest, a digging stick, a willow
basket, a reedy nest, turtle woman, Ishtar, the Great
She Bear in the sky, a raftful of sisters, starry eyed,
the Pleiades, exploding into light

—for Marie Annharte Baker

56

so, who are you anyway, where did you come from,
what do you want. stranger. why do you insist,
insist. why didn't you die, when the hammer hit,
when the door flew open, & the whiskey jacks came
flying in, their feather tips brushing against you, their
black and white wings, their unearthly cawing, their
dream of dying. what were you thinking of, stranger.
why didn't you go back, why on earth did you want
to stay. in spite of the danger, the smell of anger, the
rough taste of it on your tongue, burning your mouth
& nostrils. who are you, why are you here?

i don't want to do it anymore. too many poems
have been written. the air is filled with their noise,
Leonard Cohen's bright feathered birds, Patricia
Young's ten-year-old girls, their hair lathered in
shampoo swirls, their laughter perfect, beautiful,
& me, sitting here, aching with middle-age &
something else, something that eludes me, just
beyond the edges of this room, a sound, like the
sound the wind makes, at the end of March,
sighing its way into spring, i want to be wild &
unworded, like the wind, blowing through the bare
branches, toward open sky, i want to learn to fly,
not with Air Canada, with my own wings, arms
branching, feathering out, the sea down below,
roads & houses disappearing, the air sharp & clear,
Jerusalem rising from her desert bed to meet me,
glistening, luminous, her thousand musicians
playing love songs, the war over, all over, my
feathered hands caressing her stone hips & thighs,
her doorways opening to the fragrance of wine,
olives, feasting, the sky holding us lightly,
swooning, among clouds

little poet, how i found you again, that wild woolly
evening in spring, the leaves bursting promiscuously
from every brown branch, that incredible Manitoba
moment, brief wedge between winter & hot sun, snow
& blasting heat, & by nightfall, every tree dripping
with erotica, longing, & the sky, jealous as hell,
unattached, throwing itself against every bare field,
blasting the trees, & me, caught in the rain, imagine,
thunder the first week of May, such passion, torment,
the entire universe one big tempestuous teenager, so
much unbridled lust, so much feeling, oh, little poet,
how we loved the wind & the rain, that night, pushing
our way home against it, feet & legs wet, jeans
plastered against skin, nothing like it, all winter we
have waited for this magical moment, when the old
women turn to the wall, satisfied at last, ready to die,
& the spirits of the unborn line up just above the ozone
layer, me me *me!* jostling, elbowing, giggling into
place, for the first ripe moment, first womb opening,
to leap back, unguarded, into life, the mackerel
crowded seas, a mother's hot arms, the naked,
flamboyant trees

you wake up the old time in me, before spiders
could make us scream, *eeeeeh!* tiny terror, all
that's left to us now, these centuries later, to
remember, the heavy step at the door, black
robes, priest's fingers pointing at, the web in
the corner, the devil's sign, take her away, for
burning, every woman in the village past
childbearing age is a witch, make the daughters
watch, give them jewels & treats, so they may
listen, & learn, make the sons cut the wood, stoke
the fire, let them be strong, so they may feel lucky
to be, the chosen sons & daughters of Abraham

in the Name of the Father the Name of the Father
the Name of the Father

taming the mother blood in us, the moon magic,
impaling us with mops & brooms, against the
walls of our houses, forever & ever, dead women,
wailing inside, chanting above the flames, the
names of our lost, children

making spells, against God, against priests,
against forgetting, weaving webs of grief in the
air, millions of us, in the night sky, filigree of fire

waiting for time to bend itself around, great
heavenly wheel turning, Spider Woman,
Grandmother, reaching out her arms, to us, again,
among trees, her deep, wise wrinkling, here, here,
we are still here

—*for Thomson Highway*

& it amuses us to think that in death you're becoming
one of us, fond of ritual, & superstition, a regular old
ghost, speaking with us the language of tobacco, &
magic rings & crystal, & bits of cloth hung on trees,
on a wild riverbank, beside an old haunted graveyard,
with a bunch of crying, laughing women, how you
would have scoffed at us in life, for dabbling in
spirits, & feelings, & dreams, afraid of their power,
how temporary after all is that mighty world system
you believed in so much, unable to take you into
death, into the black night, unable to sustain you in
joy longer than it takes to count up the profits, the
harvest, next summer's grain prices, to tally up the
many, contradictory Words of God, & oh daddy,
isn't this fun, now that you're spirit & we're grown
women, wild spirited, like you, here beside this
brown river, in tall grass, lying among weeds, under
willows & sugar maples, drunk with wild blossom
scented sun, & prairie sky, & women's laughter, feet
in the air

this is probably the last poem i will write
for you, lover, ex-lover, my love, how to
gather up the threads of my longing, these
hundred days & nights, waiting for you, tie
them together in a knot, big enough to hold
me against your never coming back. these
are the last words i will write for you, tears
i will cry, sighs i will sigh. such sweetness,
such bitterness in your face & eyes, your
hot strong thighs. your mouthful of lies.

those of us who have daughters & are "so amazed,"
seeing their translucent skin & sun gilded hair,
their strong bones, & perfect lips & teeth, tossing
themselves so prodigally, carelessly, to the world,
knowing there is no end to their *perfect* beauty

those of us who bite our nails at night, counting the
minutes, after midnight, for the hour of darkness,
to pass, eventually, into dawn, the first grey light,
first twittering of birdsong

laughter, the shuffling of feet, clothes on the floor,
their eyes, so bright with knowing, everything you
know & don't yet know, their strong hands holding
all this, out, casually, to strangers, passersby

no longer babies, children, so amazed, to see them,
stepping out into daylight, their perfect anger, joy,
their bright eyes, & teeth & hair, "womb power"
surging through their limbs, the world waiting for
them, beckoning, their radiant desire

or, so appalled, not recognizing the spirit in them,
belonging to strangers, suddenly, no longer your
children, who are these changelings?

or, recognizing the spirit in them, all the contradictions
you kept hidden inside you, all those years, flaring out
in them, full blown, everything you hated, ran away
from, greeting you in their faces, how could this have
happened, there is no justice in the world, only
retribution retribution retribution

or, so much more than you deserve or could have
asked for. & yet in the end, not yours at all. just a
brief borrowing from the sky, & then, giving it all
away to earth, from the moment of conception
onwards, nothing but a leaving

don't go yet, don't go, don't go, i'm not ready for this
moment, i'm just learning how to do it right, be a mom
for you, how could it be over so soon?

knowing you will carry me in your belly forever,
across the world, knowing no matter what you wish or
decide, where you go, i will be for you, *unforgettable*

such a questionable eternity, being carried in the
daughters' bellies, with their deep rumblings, yes & no,
such a queer reversal, who would have thought it—
who would have thought any of what is

dreaming the world, a tree with heavy branches, hung
with fruit & bright feathered birds, the daughters
dancing around it, with flowers in their hair, singing
the names of their children & mothers, weaving a
chain with their singing, through the maze of time

a great circle, coming round, like the sky, its
long arm reaching across, east to west, your
life coming back to meet you, greet you, in
flashes, green, yellow, pink, against the night,
aurora borealis, the wild shivering universe,
shimmering with light, dark blue, indigo,
violet, &, that art thou, that art thou, art thou,
little one, tapping your feet on the ground,
nesting in bushes, & rocks & trees, this great
round earth, black brown, these green leaves,
these pink & yellow blossoms, opening, your
whirring, beating wings, your spirit rising,
beautiful

there is only this lake, this wind, these waves roaring,
this grey & blue, waves relentlessly pounding against
rock, against sand, hot sun beating down, waves of
heat rising from hot sand. there is only this roar,
crashing into my blood, brain, hot sun dazzling over
grey & blue water, clouds, wind, lake, sun, waves,
wind, black & white pelicans floating over the water,
in a row, their perfect symmetry, their sharp eyes, &
beaks, white gulls crying, their old grievances, old
hurt they will never forget, these great red rocks,
magnificent granite, filled with magic, singing against
heat, this fine brown sand, forgiving earth, so soft
against my feet, toes, lacy shade of young aspens,
trembling in wind, there is only this lake, these waves,
these trees, this shade, this wind, & i, am growing tree
roots, becoming gnarled, twisting among rocks,
reaching for fire, am becoming water, rock, gravel,
melting into earth, my brown skin opening, sighing,
trembling, licked by wind

making love to the spirit of the lake, on the round slope
of these red rocks, takes some courage i want you to
know! hearing among the waves the old cry of drowned
ones, sliding helplessly through deep water, the young
boaters at Grand Marais, the old fishermen, the families
of hunters crossing at Spirit Rock, whose prayers were
not good enough, the wounded outrage of gulls, herons,
no longer recognized as angels, winged spirit
messengers, the *slup, slup* of refuse & chemicals,
seeping in from drainage sewers, & the roar of the god
itself, genderless, full of fury, in spite of maps &
airplanes & motor boats, goddamn colonizers of whom
in spite of my best wishes i am one, this angry god, still
very much alive, featureless, unhuman biggest spirit i've
ever encountered, i'm filled with awe, & desire, my hot
flesh aching for this cold wet furious caress, water
pounding against sand, i'm scared, filled to overflowing
with the great furious roar of this lake, this angry god,
proud spirit, who in spite of lovers, in spite of prayers,
chemicals, spirit killers, will not be tamed, or harnessed
or subdued.

ever.

Danger lurks almost everywhere in your own house.
Fires can burn and kill. Electricity can shock. Hot water
can scald. A slippery surface can cause a fall. Knives can
cut. The list is endless. Your home is a dangerous domain.
—*Maritime Life advertisement,* Globe and Mail, *1991*

the knives in the kitchen, leaping up at me, all i was doing
was scrape the carrots, well, i thought, someone has to die,
so the rest can stay alive, it might as well be them, these
stiff orange rooted things, but they were bent on revenge,
that day, didn't want to be sliced up for soup, no way, had
their own private ideas for struggling up the developmental
chain, so they jiggled their bodies this way & that, & before
i knew it, i had a full blown revolution on my hands, every
knife in the place suddenly clattering to its feet, its
murderous impulses gleaming, blades poised for action,
well, what was i to do, i didn't want to go to work with
bandaids on every finger again, everyone laughing at me
like the last time, & me trying desperately to explain, so,
this time, i tried something else, decided to make a dance
out of it, so there we were, the carrots, the knives, & i,
pirouetting around the kitchen, oh, it was something, i tell
you, the way we dodged each other's curves, & roots &
sharp edges, making music instead of cuts & soup, & later,
i had to explain why there was no supper & we all went to
bed hungry, so that wasn't a good final solution, no , but it
worked, for one afternoon, a truce between me & the
kitchen & them, the carrots, laughing in an orange kind of
way, & me, rosy, & happy, & safe, you might say, for one
afternoon, in the dangerous domain

—*for Clarise*

she asks me which hat i'm wearing, & i'm thinking, how
treacherous, how dangerous this love is, which skirts between
mother & daughter, & lover & lover, & mentor & student, &
sister, & sister, this love which is so real, it lights up the field
of clover we're walking through, lights up also the twisted
corridors of our hard lives, which are getting easier, now, that
we're getting older, & yet so poor, it has no name, this love,
no hat to hide our heads under

i'm remembering my first image of you, drowning, how i
wanted to reach out my arm to you, hold you against the
swirling current, pull you out, onto shore

& the way you danced on the sidewalk beside me, on our way
to the art gallery, in midsummer, delighted to be there, & full of
love

& i delighted also, with you, how you'd grown, no longer
drowning, in your flowered skirt, your brown hair no longer
shaven, growing into curls

the hot sun on the clover, the humming of bees, the ache of
this poor love, without a name, our unprotected, unshaven
heads

—*for Rachel*

70

how badly she wants peace, this wise woman, this
zionist, crone, how she cries out for it, her arms
stretching out across this jagged green line, black
lines laid down, over stone, to make a place, mark
home, in this holy city, these heavenly streets, baring
her breasts in the line of fire, between these walls of
fighting men, she will not give up her dream of
Jerusalem, she will not leave, she will not close her
eyes to the pain running through each pair of dark
eyes, meeting hers in the market, the taxi, at her
apartment gate, this land that is hers, and theirs,
and ours, this land of Ishmael & Isaac, this ancient singing
land, of Asherah, that cannot be conquered or sold,
groaning to be delivered, of its love child, its
afterthought, its illegitimate offspring, sudden
tenderness in the fields of war, she holds it to her
bosom, hungrily, there, there, i have enough milk
for you, *suck*

—*for Carol Rose*

about the artist

Taysir Sharaf was born in Jerusalem in 1939. He graduated from
Alexandria University, faculty of Commerce in 1962. He is a
member of The League of Palestinian Artists, and has
participated in all the League's exhibitions from 1980 to 1990. He
has also participated in exhibitions in Amman-Jordan, Egypt,
Kuwait, United Arab Emirates, Italy, Japan and the United
States. Recently he represented the League of Palestinian Artists
in Tokyo at the "Third Word Artists Exhibition."